Knitted Animals

Licensed exclusively to Top That Publishing Ltd
Tide Mill Way, Woodbridge, Suffolk, IP12 1AP, UK
www.topthatpublishing.com
Copyright © 2014 Tide Mill Media
0 2 4 6 8 9 7 5 3 1
Printed and bound in China

Getting Started

Knitting is one of the coolest crafts around, and what could be cooler than making a collection of cute animals? When you've mastered the basic techniques explained on the next few pages, you'll find knitting relaxing, creative and, above all, fun!

Before you begin...

It's a good idea to gather together all your knitting equipment and materials before you begin, so look at the list of things you'll need at the start of each project. In addition to the knitting needles supplied, you'll need a sewing needle, a yarn needle, scissors, pins, fabric glue, a pencil and tracing paper. You'll also need a selection of craft materials including colored yarn, colored felt, stuffing, embroidery thread and decorations such as sequins, beads, buttons, ribbons and bows. You can find all of these things in craft or hobby stores, or you can buy them online.

Using templates

Each project has templates and liners for you to use. Once you're confident at knitting, you could always adapt the templates to make your own creations!

Adult help required!

While you're learning the basics of knitting, ask an adult to help you. You'll be knitting solo in no time!

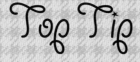

Top Tip

Keep your equipment, materials and knitting projects safely in one place, such as an old cake tin or a knitting bag. The easier it is to carry around, the better!

⚠ WARNING!

Take care when using knitting needles, sewing needles and scissors, as they have sharp points.

How to Knit

Slip knot

This will keep the yarn on your needles and also form your first stitch.

1. Make a loop at the end of your yarn.

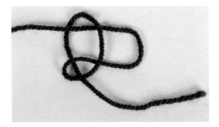

2. Create a new loop in the yarn and pull it through, as shown.

3. Carefully slip the end of one needle through the loop.

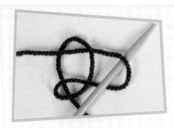

4. Pull both ends of the yarn tight to secure the knot on the needle.

Casting on

Follow these easy steps to cast on your yarn.

1. Wrap the yarn over and around your thumb, as shown.

2. Place the needle through the yarn.

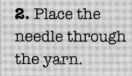

3. Pull the yarn off your thumb and onto the needle. Pull to tighten.

4. Cast on the number of stitches as shown on row one of your template.

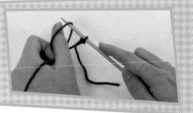

Running stitch

Tie a knot at the end of your thread. Push the needle into the fabric and back out again. Repeat until you have completed your sewing, then finish with a knot.

Knit stitch

When you are starting a new row, hold the needle with the stitches in your left hand. Knit from right to left, holding the yarn in your right hand.

3a. From above, the yarn has created a loop around each needle, as shown.

3b. Insert the right-hand needle into the front of the left-hand loop, crossing the left-hand needle.

1. Push the right-hand needle under the first stitch so the needles are crossed.

4. Pull the right-hand needle and loop off the left-hand needle. Pull the stitch tight.

2. Wrap the yarn around the right-hand needle counterclockwise (from back to front). It should lie between the two needles.

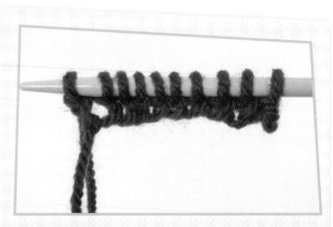

5. When you have finished a row, count the stitches to make sure you haven't dropped any. Now hold this needle in your left hand.

4

Increasing

Add an extra stitch to a row to increase your knitting.

3. Push the right-hand needle into the back of the stitch on the left-hand needle, as shown.

1. Knit one stitch as normal, but don't pull it off the left-hand needle.

4. Wrap the yarn counterclockwise around the right-hand needle. Knit the stitch off as normal, pulling it off the left-hand needle.

2. Pull the right-hand needle behind the left-hand needle, as shown.

5. You should now have two stitches on your right-hand needle.

Decreasing

Remove stitches from a row to decrease the size of your knitting.

1. Push the right-hand needle through the first two stitches on the left-hand needle.

2. Wrap the yarn counterclockwise around the right-hand needle and down through the middle.

3. Pull the right-hand needle under the stitches and to the front of the left-hand needle.

4. Pull the stitches off the left-hand needle. You should have one stitch on the right-hand needle.

Casting off

Take the stitches off the needle one by one.

1. Knit two stitches.

4. Repeat step 3 until only one stitch is on the right-hand needle.

2. Use the left-hand needle to lift the first stitch over the second stitch and off the tip of the needles.

5. Loosen the stitch and pull out the needle.

3. Knit another stitch as normal. Again use the left-hand needle to pull the first stitch over the second and off the needles.

6. Cut the yarn off the ball (leave about 4 in.) and thread the end back through the loop. Pull the thread tight to secure.

Dropped stitch

If you spot a hole in your work, you have probably dropped a stitch.

1. Knit to the end of the row. Carefully slide the knitting needle out of the stitches.

2. Gently pull the yarn, so the rows unravel to the row where you dropped the stitch. Make sure you unravel this row too.

3. Carefully push the left-hand needle through the stitches again, making sure you catch all of them, including the dropped stitch. Count to make sure! Now carry on knitting.

Sewing in ends

When your knitting is finished you can neaten it by sewing in loose ends.

1. Thread an end onto an embroidery needle.

2. Push the needle through the edge of the knitting, about five or six rows.

3. Pull the yarn through, then trim the end. Repeat with the other loose end.

Sewing up seams

Sew up pieces of knitting to create larger pieces or shapes.

1. Take a new piece of yarn and thread it onto an embroidery needle.

2. Hold the two pieces of knitting together and use running stitch (page 3) to sew along the seams to hold them together.

3. When you have sewn the whole seam, cut the yarn and use the needle to tuck both ends back into the knitting.

Templates

Follow the templates to knit the pieces for each project.

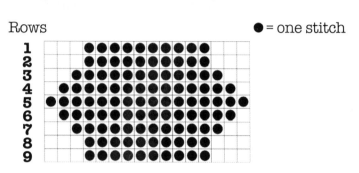

Rows　　　　　　　　● = one stitch

1. To use the template, count the number of stitches in row one.

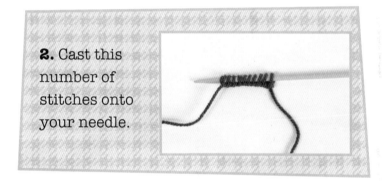

2. Cast this number of stitches onto your needle.

3. Count the number of stitches in row two. This is the number of stitches you need for your second row of knitting.

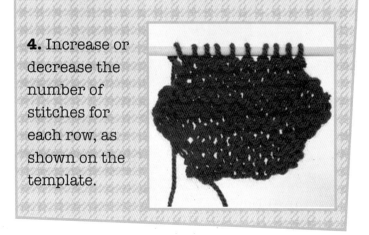

4. Increase or decrease the number of stitches for each row, as shown on the template.

Knitted Monkey

Follow these simple steps to knit a cheeky monkey fit to be a king!

You will need:

- colored yarn • knitting needles
- tracing paper • patterned fabric or felt
- pins • needle and thread
- stuffing • pipe cleaner
- scissors • fabric glue
- pencil • two buttons (optional)
- piece of ribbon • toothpick
- beads and sequins

1. First, use the body template opposite to knit two body pieces in the color you want your monkey to be.

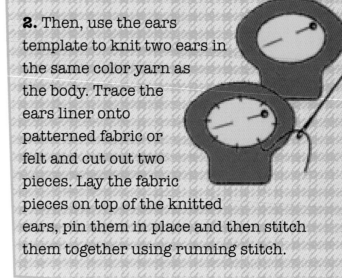

2. Then, use the ears template to knit two ears in the same color yarn as the body. Trace the ears liner onto patterned fabric or felt and cut out two pieces. Lay the fabric pieces on top of the knitted ears, pin them in place and then stitch them together using running stitch.

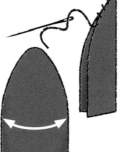

3. Knit two arms using the arms template. Fold each arm in half and stitch around the edge, as shown. Place to one side.

4. Use the feet template to knit two feet. Fold each foot in half and stitch around the edge, leaving a gap at the bottom. Fill each foot with stuffing.

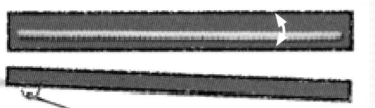

5. Knit the monkey's tail using the template. Place the pipe cleaner in the center of your knitted tail (if the pipe cleaner is too long, ask an adult to cut the end off—it should fit neatly inside the knitting). Fold the tail around the pipe cleaner and stitch along the edge to secure.

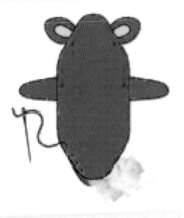

6. Lay the two body pieces on top of each other. Place the ends of each ear between the pieces and both arms about halfway down the body. Pin all of the layers together.

7. Sew along the edge of the body pieces to secure the ears and arms, as shown. Leave a small gap at the bottom where you can add stuffing.

8. Push stuffing into the monkey's body, making sure you push it up to the top of the body with your fingers. When the body is half full, tie a piece of matching yarn tightly around the middle of the body (just above the arms) to make the head.

Templates

Each dot represents the number of stitches on each row.

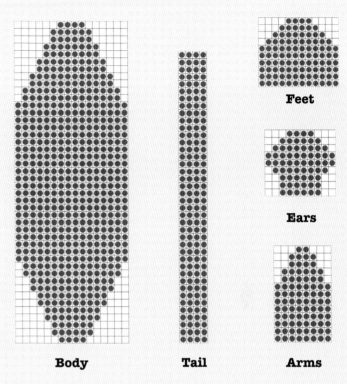

Feet

Ears

Body   **Tail**   **Arms**

Liners

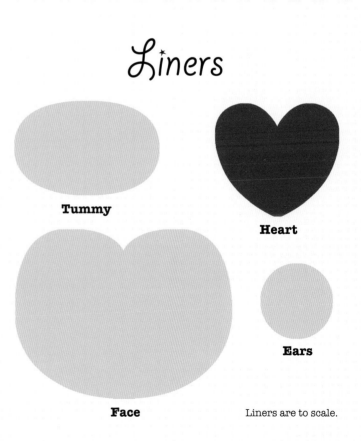

Tummy

Heart

Face   Liners are to scale.

Ears

11

9. Stuff the lower half of the body. When you think the monkey is full enough, sew up the hole at the bottom of the body.

10. Sew the feet onto either side of the front of the body, as shown. Your monkey will need these to help it balance when standing up.

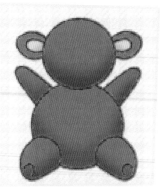

11. Sew the tail onto the back of the monkey's body. Curl the tail into the shape you want and then stitch further up the tail to hold it in place against the body.

12. Trace the face and tummy liners (page 11) onto felt and cut out. Pin the face onto the monkey's head and the tummy onto the monkey's body. Stitch them onto the monkey, as shown.

13. Cut out two small circles in a pink-colored felt for the cheeks and a black circle for the nose. Glue them in place.

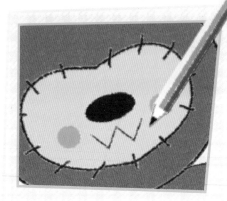

14. Using a pencil, lightly draw on the mouth. Stitch over your line using black embroidery thread.

15. Glue on black felt circles for the eyes, or stitch on two matching buttons.

16. Tie a brightly-colored piece of ribbon around the monkey's neck to hide the yarn and finish with a bow.

17. For the monkey's wand, trace and cut out two hearts (page 11) from colored felt. Sew them together, leaving a small hole at the bottom to add stuffing. Once stuffed, sew up the hole. Ask an adult to push the heart onto a toothpick, then push the other end through the monkey's hand.

Make a crown for your monkey by cutting out a long piece of felt and then cutting a zigzag pattern along the top. Add beads or sequins to the top of each spike to decorate.

Knitted Panda

This cute panda is ready for a summer vacation!

You will need:

- colored yarn • knitting needles
- tracing paper • patterned fabric or felt
- pins • needle and thread • stuffing
- scissors • fabric glue • pencil
- two buttons • piece of ribbon
- cocktail umbrella

1. Follow the body template (page 14) to knit two body pieces in the color you want your panda to be.

2. Choose another color of yarn and, using the ears template (page 14), knit two ears. Trace the ears liner onto patterned fabric or felt and cut out two pieces. Pin the fabric pieces onto the knitted ears and sew them together with running stitch.

3. Use the arms template (page 14) to knit two arms to match the ears. Fold each arm in half and stitch around the edge, as shown. Place to one side.

4. Use the feet template (page 14) to knit two feet. Fold each foot in half and stitch around the edge, leaving a gap at the bottom. Fill each foot with stuffing.

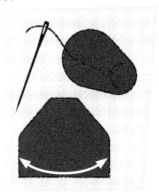

13

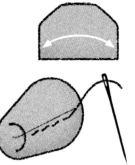

5. Knit the panda's tail, following the template (opposite), in the same color yarn as the body. Once complete, sew up the edges to secure.

6. Lay the two body pieces on top of each other. Place the ends of each ear between the pieces, and both arms about halfway down the body. Pin all of the layers together.

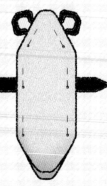

7. Sew along the edge of the body pieces. Leave a small gap at the bottom where you can add stuffing.

Templates

Each dot represents the number of stitches on each row.

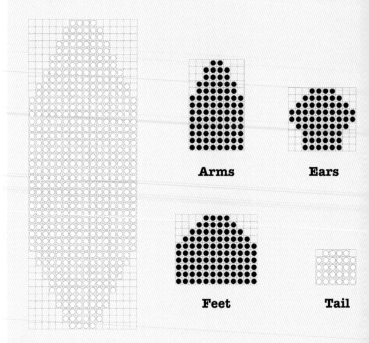

Arms

Ears

Feet

Tail

Body

Liners

Liners are to scale.

Ears

Eyes

Pocket

Face

Tummy

Apron

14

8. Push stuffing into the panda's body, making sure you push it up to the top of the body with your fingers. When the body is half full, tie a piece of matching yarn tightly around the middle of the body (just above the arms) to make the head.

9. Stuff the lower half of the body. When you are happy, sew up the hole at the bottom of the body.

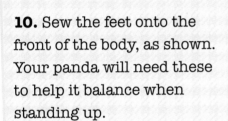

10. Sew the feet onto the front of the body, as shown. Your panda will need these to help it balance when standing up.

11. Sew the tail onto the back of the panda's body, as shown.

12. Trace the face, tummy and eye liners (opposite) onto felt and cut out (use white felt for the face, pink for the tummy and black for the eyes). Pin the face and eyes onto the panda's head, and the tummy onto the panda's body. Sew them onto the panda, as shown, using running stitch.

13. Cut out two small circles in a pink-colored felt for the cheeks and a black circle for the nose. Glue them in place.

14. Using a pencil, lightly draw on the mouth. Stitch over your line using black embroidery thread.

15. Stitch black buttons onto the eye liners for the panda's eyes.

16. Tie a brightly-colored piece of ribbon around the panda's neck to hide the yarn and finish with a bow.

Top Tips

Stitch a flower to the panda's ear to finish.

Carefully push the end of a cocktail umbrella through the panda's hand to accessorize.

Use some pretty fabric to create an apron for your panda. Trace the liner (opposite), then fold in the edges of the apron and stitch in place, creating a hem. Add the pocket in the center of the apron in a different fabric. Thread a length of ribbon through the hem at the top and gather up the apron. Use this ribbon to tie around the panda's neck to finish.

Knitted Bunny

This beautiful bunny is the perfect present to give as a gift!

You will need:

- colored yarn • knitting needles
- tracing paper • patterned fabric or felt
- pins • needle and thread • stuffing
- scissors • fabric glue • pencil
- two buttons (optional)
- piece of ribbon • bow

2. Choose another color of yarn and, using the ears template, knit the ears. Trace the ears liner onto patterned fabric or felt and cut out two pieces. Pin the fabric pieces onto the knitted ears, then sew them together with running stitch.

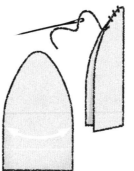

3. Use the arms template to knit two arms to match the ears. Fold each arm in half and stitch around the edge, as shown. Place to one side.

4. Use the feet template to knit two feet. Fold each foot in half and stitch around the edge, leaving a gap at the bottom to fill each foot with stuffing. Stitch to secure.

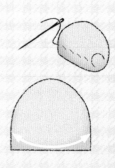

1. Use the bunny body template opposite to knit the body pieces in the color you want your bunny to be.

5. Use the tail template to knit the bunny's tail. Stitch and stuff as described in step 4.

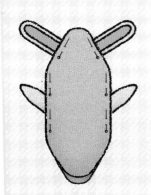

6. Lay the two body pieces on top of each other. Place the ends of each ear between the pieces and both arms about halfway down the body. Pin all of the layers together.

7. Sew along the edge of the body pieces. Leave a small gap at the bottom to add stuffing.

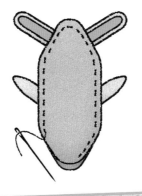

8. Push stuffing into the bunny's body. Push it up to the top of the body with your fingers. When the body is half full, tie a piece of matching yarn tightly around the middle of the body (just above the arms) to make the head.

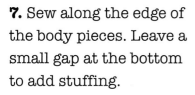

9. Stuff the lower half of the body. When you are happy, sew up the hole at the bottom of the body to secure.

Templates

Each dot represents the number of stitches on each row.

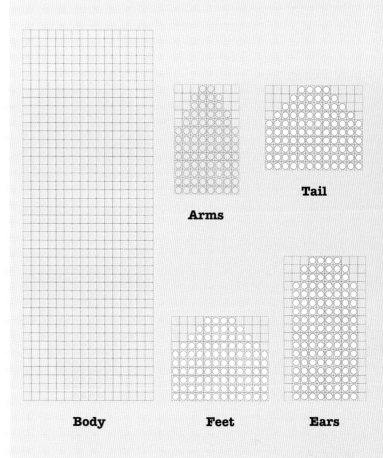

Arms

Tail

Body

Feet

Ears

Liners

Liners are to scale.

Face

Ears

Tummy

10. Sew the feet onto either side of the front of the body, as shown. Your bunny will need these to help it balance when standing up.

11. Sew the tail onto the back of the bunny's body, as shown.

12. Trace the face and tummy liners (page 17) onto felt and cut out (use the same color as the ears liner for the face and a different color for the tummy). Pin the face and tummy in place. Sew them onto the bunny, as shown, using running stitch.

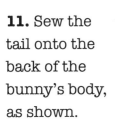

13. Cut out two small circles in a pink-colored felt for the cheeks. Glue them in place.

13a. Using a pencil, lightly draw on the nose and mouth. Stitch over the top in black embroidery thread.

13b. Cut black circles for the eyes and glue them in place, or sew on some buttons.

13c. Tie a brightly-colored piece of ribbon around the bunny's neck to hide the yarn and finish with a bow.

Top Tip

Add a bow or accessory to the bunny's ear to complete.

Knitted Bird Family

This chirpy little family is fun and easy to make! Tweet, tweet!

You will need:

- colored yarn • knitting needles
- tracing paper • patterned fabric or felt
- pins • needle and thread • stuffing
- scissors • fabric glue
- two buttons (optional)

2. Lay the two body pieces on top of each other. Sew along the edge of the pieces, leaving a small gap at the bottom to add stuffing. Once full, stitch up the hole to secure.

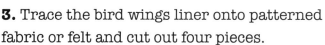

3. Trace the bird wings liner onto patterned fabric or felt and cut out four pieces.

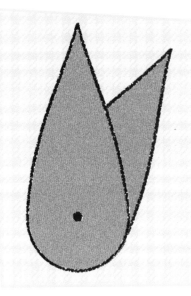

4. Place one wing piece on top of another, so you can see both pieces, as shown. Repeat to create the second wing.

1. First, use the body template (page 20) to knit two body pieces in the color you want your bird to be.

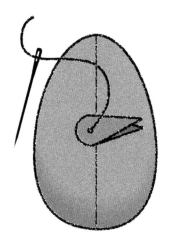

5. Place the wings on either side of the body, about halfway down, and pin in place. Using embroidery thread, stitch them onto the body with one large stitch.

6. Create some hair for the bird by stitching into the top of the head with a needle. To form loops, don't pull each stitch 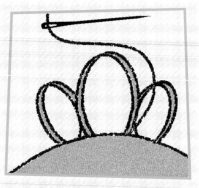 entirely through the head. Don't be afraid to experiment with the length of each loop as this will create different hairstyles.

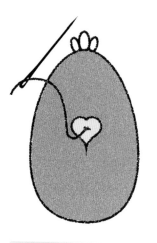

7. Trace the bird beak liner onto patterned fabric or felt and cut out the beak. Place it onto the bird's face and stitch through the center to hold in place.

8. Repeat with the bird's cheeks (using pink-colored felt). Glue in place.

9. Cut black felt circles for the eyes and glue or stitch them in place or find some small buttons and sew them in place using black embroidery thread.

Templates

Each dot represents the number of stitches on each row.

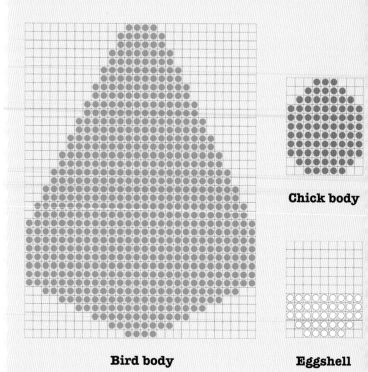

Chick body

Bird body

Eggshell

Liners

Liners are to scale.

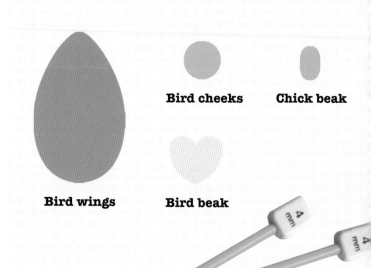

Bird cheeks

Chick beak

Bird wings

Bird beak

Chick

Use different colors of yarn to knit a big family of chirpy chicks!

1. Using the chick body template (opposite), knit two body pieces in the color of your choice.

4. Use black embroidery thread to add two eyes.

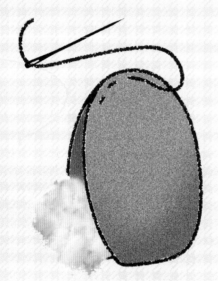

2. Lay the two body pieces on top of each other. Sew along the edge of the pieces, leaving a small gap at the bottom to add stuffing. Once full, stitch up the hole and secure.

5. Knit two eggshell pieces (see template opposite) and sew the seams together to make an egg for your chick.

3. Trace the chick beak liner onto patterned fabric or felt and cut out. Place it onto the chick's face and stitch through the center to hold in place.

21

Knitted Sheep

This cute little sheep will keep you company all day—baaaaa!

You will need:

- colored yarn • knitting needles
- tracing paper • patterned fabric or felt
- pins • needle and thread
- stuffing • scissors
- fabric glue • pencil
- two buttons (optional)
- piece of ribbon • bow

1. First, use the body template opposite to knit two body pieces in the color you want your sheep to be. Use a coarse, thick yarn if you can find some!

2. Choose a thinner yarn and, using the ears template, knit two ears. Trace the ears liner onto patterned fabric or felt and cut out the two pieces. Pin the fabric pieces onto the knitted ears and running stitch them in place, as shown.

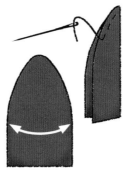

3. Use the template to knit two arms to match the ears. Fold each arm in half and stitch around the edge. Place to one side.

4. Use the feet template to knit two feet. Fold each foot in half and stitch around the edge, leaving a gap at the bottom. Stuff each foot, then stitch to secure.

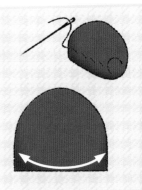

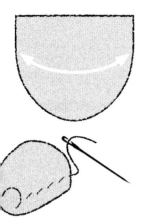

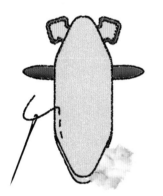

5. Knit the sheep's tail using the template. Sew up the edges and add stuffing. If your yarn is very hairy, screw an 8 in. length into a ball. Stitch through the ball to secure its shape. Place to one side.

6. Lay the two body pieces on top of each other. Place the ends of each ear between the pieces and both arms about halfway down the body. Pin all of the layers together.

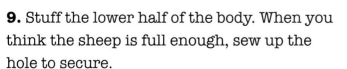

7. Sew along the edge of the body pieces. Leave a small gap at the bottom where you can add stuffing.

8. Push stuffing into the sheep's body. Push it up to the top of the body with your fingers. When the body is half full, tie a piece of matching yarn tightly around the middle of the body (just above the arms) to make the head.

9. Stuff the lower half of the body. When you think the sheep is full enough, sew up the hole to secure.

Templates

Each dot represents the number of stitches on each row.

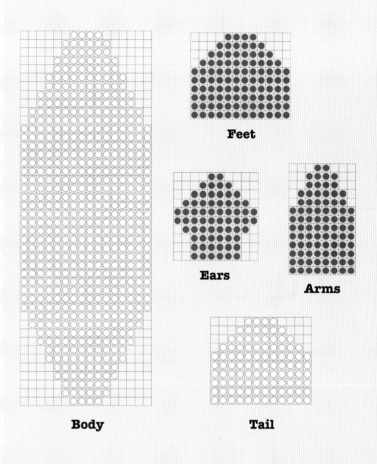

Feet

Ears

Arms

Body

Tail

Liners

Liners are to scale.

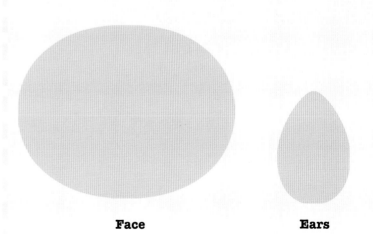

Face

Ears

10. Sew the feet onto either side of the front of the body, as shown. Your sheep will need these to help it balance when standing up.

11. Stitch your tail onto the back of the sheep's body, as shown.

15. Cut out black felt circles for the eyes and stitch them in place, or find some buttons and sew them on.

12. Trace the face liner (page 23) onto felt and cut out (use the same color as the ear liner). Pin the face onto the sheep's head and sew in place with running stitch.

16. Tie a brightly-colored piece of ribbon around the sheep's neck to hide the yarn and finish with a bow.

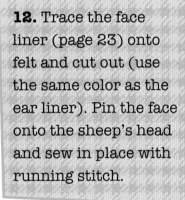

13. Cut out two small circles in a pink-colored felt for the cheeks. Glue them in place.

17. Cut an 8 in. length of yarn. Screw it into a ball with your fingers and stitch to secure its shape. Sew this to the sheep's head to give him a tuft of hair.

14. Using a pencil, lightly draw on the nose and mouth. Stitch over the top in black embroidery thread.

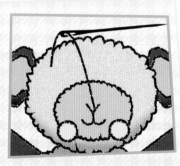

Top Tips

To finish, add a bow to the sheep's head.

Make the bow around the sheep's neck using multiple ribbons in different colors.